Series Editor: Rosalind Kerven

© 1996 Rigby Education
Published by Rigby Interactive Library,
an imprint of Rigby Education,
division of Reed Elsevier, Inc.
500 Coventry Lane,
Crystal Lake, IL 60014

Printed in Hong Kong

00 99 98 97 96
10 9 8 7 6 5 4 3 2 1

*Library of Congress Cataloging-in-Publication Data*

Branford, Henrietta, 1946–.
        The theft of Thor's hammer / retold by Henrietta Branford;
     illustrated by Dave Bowyer.
          p.    cm. — (Myths and legends)
        Summary: The Norse gods Thor and Loki descend to earth in disguise
     to regain Thor's magic hammer that has been stolen by the frost
     giant Thrym.
        ISBN 1-57572-014-0 (library)
        1. Thor (Norse deity)—Juvenile literature. [1. Thor (Norse
     deity) 2. Loki (Norse deity) 3. Mythology, Norse.] I. Bowyer,
     Dave, ill. II. Title. III. Series: Myths and legends (Crystal
     Lake, Ill.)
     BL890.T5B73    1996
        398'.2'0948'01—dc20                                          95-38242

*Acknowledgments*
Title page, border, and map, pp. 2–3: Dave Bowyer;
photograph, p. 3: Werner Forman Archive

# The Theft of Thor's Hammer

Retold by Henrietta Branford
Illustrated by Dave Bowyer
Series Editor: Rosalind Kerven

# About the Vikings

The Vikings were farmers and fishermen from the cold northern countries of Norway, Sweden, and Denmark. Over a thousand years ago, they traveled to other countries to seize land and treasure.

We know about the Vikings' lives because of the things they left behind—especially their stories.

The World of Viking Mythology

ASGARD – the home of the warrior gods

BIFROST – the rainbow bridge

MIDGARD – the earth where humans and giants live

YGGDRASIL – the tree keeping the worlds in place

NIFLHEIM – the land of the dead

## Some Viking Gods

◀ Thor was the most popular Viking god. He was big and strong, but not very clever. Thor had an awful temper, but he was fair.

Loki was a trickster who could change his shape. He especially liked turning himself into a fly. ▶

Freya was the goddess of birth and death. She was a powerful magician. ▶

Thor had a magic hammer called Miollnir (MY-oll-near). When Thor threw Miollnir, he never missed, and it flew right back into his hand. Although it was used to bless people on special occasions, it could also kill. Vikings wore little Miollnir charms like this one to keep them safe. ▶

Thor Thunder God, mighty fighter, giant beater,
felt with his huge hand for Miollnir.
Mighty Miollnir, battle hammer of the gods, was gone!
Thor shook himself, and bellowed.
Sparks flew from his red hair and his beard bristled.
Without Miollnir, Thor could not protect the gods.

"Wake up Loki!" thundered Thor.
"Help me! My hammer's gone!"
"Your thunder hurts my head," grumbled Loki.
"But I'll help you.
For with your hammer in your hand,
you are the champion of the gods.
Without it, we are all in danger."

Loki ran to visit Freya and told her
what had happened.
"Lend me your magic feather cloak," he begged.
I must fly far and fast to find Miollnir!"
"Then take it," said Freya. "Hurry!"

Loki put on the cloak and dived down from Asgard.
Down he flew to Midgard, far below, where the
giants live.
Horrible Thrym, the frost giant, sat on a hill there,
making golden leashes for his hunting dogs.
He looked up and saw Loki coming.

"What brings you down to the land of giants, Loki?"
asked Thrym.

"Is something wrong in Asgard?"

"I think you know what's wrong," said Loki.

"Tell me, was it you who stole Thor's hammer?"

Thrym smiled coldly.

"Thor's hammer is buried eight miles deep,"
he said. "Shall I tell you what
will make me give it back?"

Loki nodded.

"I want lovely Freya for my wife.
I must have her, and you must bring her to me!"

Loki spread out Freya's magic feather cloak
and flew away, back to Asgard.
Thor was waiting eagerly for news.
"Quick, Loki!" thundered Thor.
"Tell me! What have you found out?"
Loki told him, and they rushed to Freya's palace.

"Make yourself beautiful, Freya," Loki laughed.
"Giant Thrym wants you to be his bride."
"Marry that ice pile?" Freya screamed.
"Marry Thrym? Me? Never! Not in a million years!"
She was so angry that she burst her famous necklace.
Gold snapped, and jewels bounced like hail
upon the palace floor.

The gods and goddesses held a solemn meeting.
No one could think of how to get Thor's hammer back.
Night fell, the great hall grew dark,
and still they talked.
At last the watchman of the gods spoke up.
He knew the answer.
"Thor must go in Freya's place.
He will make a lovely bride," he said.

"Think of it, Thor.
You shall wear a wedding veil."
"I won't!" roared Thor. "And you can't make me!"
The watchman winked.
"I think a long dress would be best," he said,
"to hide your hairy legs.
And you must have fine brooches
and a pretty hat."

"Why should I?" Thor scowled.

"Why should I dress up for you to laugh at me?"

"You've got no choice," said Loki.

"Your hammer blesses all new brides.

It can give life or death.

With it, the giants will take over Asgard!"

They dressed Thor carefully.
He looked quite beautiful with his long dress,
soft veil, and all.
Loki was to be the bridesmaid.
He put on his own dress and twirled around.

The goats that pulled Thor's chariot
were quickly caught and harnessed.
Fire flew from their speeding hooves,
and the earth shook as Thor and Loki
dashed down to the land of giants.

16

Greedy Thrym looked up and saw them in the sky.
"Clean up my hall!
Get the feast ready," he shouted to his servants.
"Jump to it! My bride-to-be is coming.
Lovely Freya!
She's all I need to make me happy!"

What a magnificent feast!
And what an unusual bride!
She ate a whole ox, ears and all.
And then eight silver salmon, each one bigger
than the last.
She finished off the wedding cake
and drank up all the wine.
Thrym watched in wonder.
"Look at that woman eat!" he sighed.
"How does she do it?"

Clever Loki knew just what to say.
"It's because she loves you so much," he whispered.
"She hasn't eaten for a week,
just thinking of her wedding!"

Thrym couldn't wait.

He leaned in close to kiss the bride.

Suddenly he jumped backward,

right across the hall.

"Her eyes are on fire!" he yelped.

"Why are her eyes so bright?"

"Oh, she's mad about you," clever Loki told him.

"She hasn't slept for a week just thinking about you."

"Wonderful woman!" shouted Thrym.
"Let's get on with the wedding.
Bring out the hammer of the gods,
the one they always use to bless the bride!"
Mighty Miollnir was carried in
and laid gently across the bride's wide lap.
The ceremony began.

Thor jumped up and tore off his veil.
Thrym stared at him.
He could not believe what he saw.
Thor grabbed Miollnir.
He swung it high around his head
and shook it.
Mighty Miollnir was ready for battle!

Thor ran through the great hall,
pounding the wedding guests with his thunderbolts.
Giant Thrym died first.
The others followed.
The roof fell in, the tables tipped,
food flew, dogs snapped and guzzled.
Thor Thunderer destroyed them all.

Loki and Thor are home in Asgard now.
Thrym's hall, a smoking wreck, lies far below.
Mighty Miollnir is back where it belongs,
and all the gods are safe.

27 Jul 99